VIKING

INTERNET MARKETING

Chapter 1:
What is Internet Marketing?

The term "internet marketing" has become associated with a broad range of topics in recent years. For many, it literally means only what it says: "marketing on the internet", in which case it is seen as synonymous with "digital marketing" and "online marketing". For others, however, it has come to be associated more specifically with the worlds of affiliate marketing, information products, and the "make money online" niche. For our purposes, we'll lean more towards the former and will settle on the following definition:

Internet marketing is the use of internet properties and traffic to generate leads, sales, or brand awareness. This is typically done via search engine visibility, social media marketing, email marketing, and various forms of paid advertising.

One of the best ways to begin understanding internet marketing is to break down the various goals a business can seek to accomplish with it. The ultimate end goal of marketing is, of course, revenue. With that in mind, we can certainly classify sales as a primary goal of internet marketing and many businesses do focus on sending traffic directly to paid offers, whether digital product sales pages or physical product pages in an eCommerce store. However, for many businesses, sales remain a distant, long term goal. A more common immediate or short-term goal of internet marketing, however, is lead generation. By using the internet to affordably collect leads rather than make individual sales, a business can then use their lead list to continue marketing for free (or close to free) to potential customers from that point forward with the expectation that multiple future sales will increase the average lifetime value of each lead and result in a greater long-term ROI from each dollar spent on marketing.

Lead generation for an online business might consist simply of building an email list, perhaps with customer names associated as well. Lead generation for an eCommerce business or local "offline" business might also include physical mailing addresses and phone numbers so they can follow up in other ways such as telemarketing or mailing out catalogues and special offers. Other businesses might pursue even more robust lead data such as business information like industry categories or number of employees in the case of B2B marketing, or income ranges and family size in the case of higher-ticket B2C models like insurance sales or real-estate. Since lead generation is often seen as the most common and multi-faceted immediate goal of internet marketing, the entirety of chapter three will be devoted to the various methods and forms of lead generation.

Finally, another immediate goal of internet marketing is growing brand awareness and familiarity. For many businesses, this might consist of spending large amounts on banner advertisements or video ads primarily for the purpose of getting their brand name, logo, or unique selling proposition

(USP) in front of as many eyes as possible as many times as possible. The idea here is to increase top-of-mind awareness so that the potential customer will think of the brand in future situations when they need that specific need fulfilled. For example, when a fast food chain airs ads on television, it's not because they expect people to immediately hop in the car and go buy a burger because of it. It's because they want you to think of their restaurant next time you clock-out for your lunch break and are deciding what to eat. The internet marketing equivalent of this might be an online tax service heavily investing in banner ads and video ads in December and January, not because they think people will suddenly start doing their taxes early, but because in April when 90% of Americans do their taxes at the last minute, their brand will be the first one they remember. Other forms of brand awareness might simply consist of frequent social media posting. Companies know that constantly seeing their brand image in their followers' newsfeeds or Twitter feeds accomplishes that same top-of-mind awareness as well as other emotional associations with their brand such as loyalty, pride, good will, and humor (covered in more detail in Chapter two).

Chapter 2:

Internet Marketing Methods

Regardless of whether your intended destination for traffic is a sales page, a lead page, or simply a piece of content, the potential internet marketing methods are manifold. We'll cover the most common ones here.

Email Marketing

Email marketing is unique in this list for a very obvious reason: you already have their email address. In other words, the main goal of email marketing is sales, whereas the other methods in this list can have both sales and lead generation as a goal. Email marketing basically consists of sending promotional email messages to a list of leads, typically using an autoresponder service like GetResponse or Aweber. Email marketing can be done on a completely manual basis, in which a business sends out newsletters or offers at their respective times, or on an automatic basis, in which a list of leads are put through a sequence of pre-planned auto-responder messages.

More recently, the concept of marketing automation has become popular. This is where leads are put through a unique series of autoresponder sequences that change and adapt based on the actions of the lead and various "if this then that" (IFTTT) conditions established by the marketer. For example, if a lead does not open an email, they might be automatically sent a follow-up email asking why they hadn't opened the previous one, or if a lead clicks on a certain link in an email which indicates they have a particular interest, they might be segmented into a separate list or new sequence that caters to that specific interest.

SEM

Search Engine Marketing consists of leveraging a search engine's paid advertising platform to position your business as a "sponsored" search result in a prominent, visible place on Search Engine Results Pages (SERPs). The most popular search engines for SEM at the moment are Google and Bing. A business can setup their ad to target a group of keywords that they'd like to "rank" for, as well as selecting other variables such as demographics and location. These ads will then appear at the top or bottom of the SERPs (depending on various factors such as budget and bidding) and will have the appearance of a typical search result, with the one exception of a small word like "ad" or "sponsored" somewhere on it (this varies among search engines).

SEO

Search Engine Optimization is the use of various on-site and off-site practices and factors to make your web properties rank higher in search results. These practices include methods like keyword usage, original content, frequent updating/posting, backlinking, social sharing, bounce rates (how many people leave after viewing just one page), visitors' average time on site, and the use of images and videos. Until around 2012, SEO was arguably considered the most vital internet marketing method around and, depending on your industry, it might still be.

However, in recent years the growing number of competing web properties in the online space have made ranking very difficult and expensive for many businesses. This, along with constant changes to some of the top search engines' algorithms have led many businesses to conclude that paid SEM is more cost-effective than SEO. SEO still maintains its importance in many cases, however, such as in the case of local "brick and mortar" businesses whose search rankings are positively affected by the use of nearby city names in the search terms as well as the various search engines' use of locational data.

Ad Networks

Ad networks are an excellent way to get your brand or offer in front of your target audience on a broad range of web properties. The most commonly discussed ad network is Google's AdWords network but there are several other out there. Using these networks will allow you to place banner image ads, video ads, or simple textual ads in front of web traffic on a variety of websites. This approach can be especially powerful when combined with retargeting. This entails placing retargeting pixels on your web properties and then specifically targeting your site visitors via ad networks so that the offer they initially looked at (and are presumably interested in) starts following them around the internet wherever they go. This may sound creepy, but statistics indicate that people who are retargeted are 70% more likely to convert!

Individual Sites

Some marketers might prefer to do their advertising on a case-by-case basis by personally approaching individual, relevant websites, forums, or blogs in their niche or industry. When using this manual method, marketers should be sure to research the metrics of the given site, blog, or forum. Naturally you'll want to display your ad in places with a reasonable level of traffic and a positive reputation to ensure your advertising dollars are spent well. You can learn a lot about websites by researching them on Alexa. That said, the majority of businesses tend to find the use of ad networks to be a more cost-effective way of advertising.

Social Media Marketing

Social media marketing has come a long way in the last several years and has changed the way many businesses think about marketing in general. For some marketers, social followers have replaced email addresses, posts and tweets have replaced promotional emails, and likes have replaced email opens. Virtually every successful business today has not only a social media presence, but a clearly defined social media strategy. Most of these strategies revolve around posting consistent content.

But it's more than just posting promotions and offers. A successful social strategy will include various types of non-promotional content for various types of goals. Posting about a charitable cause associates your brand with feelings of goodwill. Posting about trendy topics makes your brand seem relevant. Posting useful tips without a sales pitch makes your business come off as genuinely helpful. Posting humorous or "feel-good" content associates your business with positive emotions, and so on. But more importantly, these types of non-promotional posts are accomplishing two other goals. First, they're encouraging social sharing, which grows your following even more. Secondly, they're creating top-of-mind awareness for your brand. People will get used to seeing your content and your business name, logo, and USP. As a result, when they have a problem that your business fixes, they'll be more likely to think of you first.

All of those social media concepts revolve around organic activity. However, the major social media platforms today have also developed robust paid advertising systems. The most game-changing of these has been the concept of social "native advertising". Native advertising refers to advertisements that have the appearance of organic content with the exception of a tiny one-word disclaimer somewhere designating it as "sponsored" or an "advertisement". This new form of paid social media advertising has proven to be remarkably effective because social media consumers are already in the habit of looking at, consuming, and engaging with anything that looks like an organic post in their social feeds. In addition to this, the line between organic posts and paid native ads have become increasingly blurred as these native ads act and function just like organic content (they can be shared, liked, etc.) and businesses now have the ability to pay to promote an organic post to give it further reach.

Video Marketing

If there's one thing that has been well established in marketing today, it's the tremendous power of video. Nothing else compares. Understandably then, marketers have seized on video and are leveraging it in numerous ways. Video marketing is often executed as social media marketing. Businesses are publishing video content on multiple video sites such as YouTube, DailyMotion, and Vimeo just as they would publish non-video content to Facebook or Twitter.

As with the social media strategy described earlier, a successful video content strategy includes a good mix of useful, helpful, trending, humorous, and "feel-good" video content, with "salesy" videos being in the minority. Once published, video content should be cross-promoted on other social media platforms to increase exposure. Another recent development is that major social networks like Facebook and Twitter have added their own video uploading and streaming functions, increasing the overlap between video marketing and social media marketing.

One further angle on video marketing is paid video advertising. Presently, the most popular version of this is YouTube/AdWords video ads which appear at the beginning of videos on both YouTube as well as other video-playing properties around the web. These video ads can typically be skipped after several seconds. In addition to the YouTube/AdWords video ad network, businesses also often pay for video ads on an individual basis on other websites, news sites, and so on.

Content Marketing

Content marketing is largely included in the other marketing methods mentioned thus far, but it's also worth discussing by itself. The most common forms of content marketing are blog posts, news articles, and social posting, but content marketing can also include video and image publishing. The goals of content marketing are manifold. Firstly, it builds goodwill with followers who associate your brand with helpful content. Secondly, content marketing provides an opportunity to hide a "soft pitch" within "non-salesy" content which can lead to sales while at the same time providing useful content. Thirdly, content marketing can be an excellent way to "pixel" an audience for later retargeting which has proven to be a devastatingly effective tactic. Finally, content is the primary driver in most search engines' algorithms which can result in higher rankings. There are many benefits beyond these four, but these can be considered the most relevant and directly impactful ones.

Old School Methods

The following methods have largely become less common, if not altogether abandoned, because of negative connotations or even penalties that have been attached to them in the past. Bit since it's theoretically possible to engage in these in a non-spammy manner, it's worth mentioning them briefly. Blog commenting and video commenting can often be an effective way to get your brand in front of relevant audiences. Just make sure that your comments are relevant, useful, and not spammy and definitely do not mass-post comments for the sake of backlinking as that will likely kill your SEO thanks to recent search engine algorithms designed to penalize abusers of this tactic.

Forum posting is another marketing method that has become less popular today. However, this was less due to abuses (although there certainly were some) and more towards a drifting away towards social media platforms. It simply become more cost-effective and fruitful to focus on social media. However, it is often the case that most of the serious devotees of a certain niche may be more likely to be found on niche-related forums, which means it can still be beneficial to market your brand in the signature section of your posts and interact on relevant forums periodically. Just make sure you're making genuine and sincere contributions to the conversation.

Chapter 3:
Internet Lead Generation

Most of the above marketing methods have the same immediate goal in mind: getting traffic to a web page. This web page could be either a sales/order page or a lead generation page. Since sales is a relatively straightforward topic and lead generation is at the forefront of immediate internet marketing goals, we'll be focusing on all the variations of lead generation.

Email List Building

At the top of the lead generation list is email list building. They say "the money is in the list" and it's true. The most common method of email list building is to send traffic to a lead generation page of some sort. Typically, this is a landing page pitching some sort of free offer or "lead magnet" in exchange for a person typing their email into an opt-in form. This opt-in form might also ask for a name, since personalized subject lines are known to increase open rates by around 30%. In addition to a traditional opt-in form which often sadly leads to low quality email addresses that are rarely checked or even fake names and emails, there are two recent developments that have allowed marketers to increase the quality of the contact info they collect.

The first of these developments is the "lead ad" or "lead card" concept available on Facebook and Twitter's advertising platforms. This newer type of ad pre-fills Facebook and Twitter users' name and email in the opt-in form, and requires them only to tap the submit button. This is beneficial because the emails and names associated with a person's social media account are more likely to be real and regularly checked. That said, many people set up their social accounts many years ago, and no longer check those email addresses regularly and users can still choose to click on and change the auto filled data in those fields to a "secondary", rarely checked, or even fake email address. This weakness has led to yet another solution designed to maximize lead quality and email open rates: Warlord Mobile Leads.

Warlord Mobile Leads is a tool that ensures that you get a person's primary email address and real name without them having to type anything into an opt-in form. It does this by leveraging the email app on their mobile device and has become an increasingly popular list building option since 2016 due to the fact that most traffic these days is coming from mobile devices.

Robust Lead Generation

For businesses that require a bit more lead data, a more robust lead collection approach may be necessary. This simply entails adding more fields to an opt-in form. Depending on a business' needs, this may include items such as phone numbers, mailing addresses, business names, industries, income levels, family size, and so on.

SMS List Building

Text Message Marketing has become increasingly popular in recent years. Initially, the main use of SMS list building was for major retailers to send out special coupons and promotional messages. However, more recently, many online businesses have been leveraging SMS messaging for things such as webinar reminders and sales promotions. There are various ways of conducting this type of list building, including having people input their mobile numbers or having them send a text message to a special number.

Push Notifications

An even more recent trend has been to have people opt in to push notifications. This involves a pop-up on your website requesting permission to send people future updates directly via their browsers. When a person consents to this, you are then able to send notifications that pop up in a box on the bottom right of their screen at any time in the future.

Retargeting

Building a retargeting audience can be considered another form of list building and is relatively easy to do. Various platforms including AdRoll, Facebook, Twitter, and many others have a retargeting pixel that you can paste onto your web properties. Once this is done, all traffic to these pages will be cookied and added to your retargeting list. From that point forward, you'll have the ability to place your ads in front of these people almost anywhere on the web. This includes on social platforms like Facebook, Twitter, and Instagram, video sites like YouTube, and virtually any website, news site, blog, or forum that participates in any of the major online ad networks. This is a very valuable form of lead generation because retargeted traffic has been shown to convert at a 70% higher rate than cold traffic.

Social Followers

Finally, building a social following can be considered another form of lead generation. With a large enough social following, a business can post to one of the major social networks and have their content and promotions seen in the social feeds of countless potential customers. The possibility of these followers sharing these posts gives businesses yet another way to expand their list even further. Some social networks, like Facebook, have recently decreased the percentage of a business' audience that will see organic posts in their news feeds. However, if an audience is large enough, social posting remains a powerful form of marketing today.

Chapter 4:
Internet Marketing Tools

Regardless of which method of lead generation you focus on, your business will need a host of tools to generate leads. For email list building, you'll require a minimum of two tools: an autoresponder and a landing page builder. Your autoresponder will be the platform where your email list is sent, stored, and communicated with. Your landing page builder, on the other hand, will be where you place your opt-in forms and collect your leads.

Popular autoresponders include:

GetResponse
Aweber
SendReach
Constant Contact
Active Campaign
MailChimp

Popular landing page builders include:

InstaPage
LeadPages
OptimizePress
InstaBuilder
Thrive Themes

For those hoping to collect higher quality leads and to ensure that they collect real names and primary email addresses, the appropriate tool for this is Warlord Mobile Leads.

For businesses that require more robust lead generation data, this can usually be done with the above-mentioned autoresponders and landing page builders. However, for more flexible and wide ranging forms, a business might find that a service like FormSite.com, Wufoo, or Formstack will fill their needs better.

There are a variety of potential tools for **SMS list building** including:

TextDeliver
Twilio
Trumpia

Push-notifications can be accomplished with multiple tools including:

PushCrew
Push Connect Notify
OneSignal

Retargeting can be accomplished via various platforms such as:

Facebook
Twitter
Google AdWords
AdRoll
Perfect Audience

Finally, social media marketing can easily be done via the various social platforms themselves. However, many marketers prefer to rely on social media management tools such as:

Warlord Social Suite
HootSuite
OnlyWire

Battle Plan

So, you've just sat through one of the most detailed and up to date internet marketing guides available. But guess what? Everything you've learned here counts for nothing if you don't immediately start applying it. Have a look at the battle plan below and start implementing these steps today.

Step 1: Determine your most important internet marketing goals.

Step 2: Choose 2 or 3 marketing methods to focus on.

Step 3: Acquire the necessary tools to employ those methods.

Step 4: Start implementing your internet marketing strategy immediately.

www.ingramcontent.com/pod-product-compliance
Lightning Source LLC
Chambersburg PA
CBRC090851210326
41597CB00011B/170